SUCH IS THE WAY OF THE WORLD

SUCH IS THE WAY OF THE WORLD

A Journey through Grief

Barbara Schiff Brisson

PAULIST PRESS
NEW YORK/MAHWAH, N.J.

COVER & TEXT DESIGN BY JAMES F. BRISSON

Copyright © 1997 by Barbara Schiff Brisson

All rights reserved. No part of this book may be reproduced or transmitted in any form or by any means, electronic or mechanical, including photocopying, recording or by any information storage and retrieval system without permission in writing from the Publisher.

Library of Congress Cataloging-in-Publication Data

Brisson, Barbara Schiff.
   Such is the way of the world : a journey through grief / Barbara Schiff Brisson.
      p.   cm.
   ISBN 0-8091-3691-0 (alk. paper)
   1. Bereavement—Psychological aspects. 2. Bereavement—Religious aspects—Christianity. 3. Grief. 4. Grief—Religious aspects—Christianity. 5. Loss (Psychology) I. Title.
   BF575.G7B737 1996
   155.9'37—dc20
                                                  96-29384
                                                           CIP

Published by Paulist Press
997 Macarthur Boulevard
Mahwah, New Jersey 07430

Printed and bound in the United States of America

This book is dedicated to the loving memory of
BERTHA ANNA MARIE ORTMAN ALLEN
July 19, 1881—July 15, 1981

My greatest teacher
Who opened my heart to the love of the Bible
and the joy of gardens.
Whose patience and kindness
taught me compassion and love.

May her spirit always shine like a beacon
throughout my life.

BARBARA SCHIFF BRISSON

CONTENTS

PREFACE • IX

INTRODUCTION • XI

1. Death as Transformation
   and Change • 1

2. Grief and the Grieving Process • 13

3. The Healing Process • 30

4. A Time to Heal • 56

5. Transformation as Growth—
   Ways to Heal Yourself and
   Help Others • 73

PREFACE

When the angels came down to earth to announce the birth of Jesus to the shepherds, they said:

"Fear not, for I bring you tidings of great joy!"

Now, they could have started with "Hallelujah" or "Glory Be" or "Praise God," but they didn't. They said, "**Fear not**," because fear would stop even the interaction with the *angels*.

So I say unto you, "Fear not, this book will also bring you tidings and I hope, eventually, great joy. So fear not!"

INTRODUCTION

This book came about because of a letter. I heard of someone in a most difficult situation. While his mother was visiting she had a serious heart attack and was rushed into the hospital for surgery. When his father, at home in another state far away, heard of his wife's condition, he suffered a massive heart attack and died. This was tragic. How could a healing begin in the chaos of emotions and worry? I knew that in long time marriages or relationships a heart bond or heart connection grows that transcends time and space. Love is a powerful force. Here was a case of someone not being able to live without his lifetime partner. The old adage that if you love someone you will let them go first resounded in my head. This was love at its most forceful. Perhaps if the family could see the dynamics behind this tragedy, a healing could happen. So I wrote a letter.

That letter came into the hands of Karen Scialabba who called me. After a series of long talks, she encouraged me to write a book about the dynamics at work in the process of mourning. If it weren't for Karen's persistence and encouragement, this book would have remained just a letter. As my editor, Karen has guided me with insightful and capable hands.

The form of a book is as important as its content. That this book is easy to read, easy on the eyes and beautiful inside and out is due to the designer, James F. Brisson. I am eternally grateful for all his help and patience. This would never have become a book without him.

CHAPTER 1

Death as Transformation and Change

*"Experience is not what happens to you;
it is what you do with what happens to you."*
—ALDOUS HUXLEY

TRANSFORMATION means more than "to change." It is to build anew with what you already have and know. Transform: to cross over from, to re-form into something completely new. It is a journey from the familiar to the unknown. It is nothing less than rebirth. For every loss there is re-growth. One can mark the changes, like milestone markers along the way.

I often think death is like being on a commercial airline. There's lots of preparation before the trip and, for me at least, anxiety. Once the plane takes off there's no going back, no change of mind, no way to say, "Stop! I want to get off!" Whether I like it or not, I'm there for the ride. I trust and pray that I will make it safely to my destination, but no matter what, there is nothing I can do. The adventure has begun and it is out of my hands. Now, I acknowledge that my decision to begin the journey was my choice, but for the duration of the trip, my life is not in my control. I can only wait until the plane lands. What sustains me is that others fly all the time and most get through it. I feel that way about death and grief, too. It happens to others all the time and most get through it one way or another.

I'm amazed at how little preparation is given in life for grief and loss, something each of us must go through many times in life. We are given more training before we get a license to drive a car! Yet grief paralyzes us in our lives. How do we get through it?

I'd like to answer neatly that there are so many steps and such and such procedures, but grief is a personal thing that almost all human beings (and many animals) share in common. Dr. Elisabeth Kübler-Ross has given us the steps in her book *Death and Dying*: Denial, Depression, Anger, Bargaining and Acceptance. Surely we go through these steps as well when dealing with grief. The difference is that death can often cut short the above process; for example, the dying person can still be in total denial when death comes and never proceed to any other stage. Grief, on the other hand, takes its own time and works through to a completion. It may take several years, but the mourner will have the rest of a lifetime to work through the grief.

As humans, we have many varied paths that our grieving takes, with just one thing in common: we all want it over with as quickly as possible.

Grieving is being in that tight space. We're miserable and uncomfortable and unhappy and all we want is OUT.

I am reminded of the Children of Israel living in slavery in Egypt, which in Hebrew is *mitzrayim* (literally, "a tight place"). Life started out in Egypt as a blessing. Jacob brought his sons and their families to Joseph because of the famine in the land of Canaan. Here Egypt was life to Jacob's vast family. Only little by little did it turn to slavery. The Egyptians' fear of the Israelites made the slavery more and more bitter. The once safe haven of Egypt became uncomfortable and miserable and unhappy. Only then did the Israelites want to leave, and not all wanted to go. What stopped some of them from not wanting to leave slavery behind was fear—fear of the unknown. Fear of the new life awaiting, the new world they would have to enter. Living in a tight place, *mitzrayim*, was better than living with fear.

Even after seeing the great wonders and miracles of the ten plagues, many were afraid of the future away from the life they had known. They were afraid of the transformation that was to come. Even with Jehovah God leading them as a pillar of smoke by day and a column of fire by night, they were still so afraid of wandering in the wilderness that many wanted to return to Egypt, saying that bitter slavery was better than this unknown. Death awaited almost all of these people. Only Joshua and Caleb, the two scouts who had no fear, made it into the Promised Land. Forty years of wandering and death for what? For transformation. The Israelites who left the desert were no longer slaves, but strong tribe units able to conquer a new land.

So it is with grief. We wander through the wilderness leaving behind forever the former self and eventually emerging a new warrior self, or at least a different self. Some of us may want to go back, but we must push forward, even if we wind up going in circles for a while.

We are the caterpillar inside that chrysalis waiting

to emerge a butterfly. Perhaps the caterpillar is perfectly happy being a caterpillar or even wants to go back after being inside that "tight" chrysalis, but it will emerge as a butterfly, or not emerge at all!

Now I'm going to propose something radical. Simply, grieving takes time. It shouldn't be rushed. If the Children of Israel took forty years, why shouldn't we be allowed a year or more for our transformations? More harm is done by the Puritan, stoic ethic of "life goes on" and "I'm just fine, thank you." I cringe every time I hear someone say, "It has been six months; why aren't they over it?"

Grief isn't bound by our time schedules. It sneaks up at odd moments. One needs, at the very least, an entire year cycle to feel the loss. A first birthday, or anniversary, or Thanksgiving, or family reunion without the loved one will bring on the flood of grief. Thoughts of the missing person will bring all the emotions of the loss, even if it is being shared lovingly.

Be gentle with yourself and with others. Allow yourself this time to weep, to laugh, to sleep, to be depressed, to read, or watch TV, or not even want to get out of bed! We all react differently to stress. A day reading a Regency romance novel won't hurt anyone and can take one off into another world for a few hours. It worked wonders for me and the world didn't stop spinning because I needed that break.

Depression is a "time-out" from dealing with the world. All troubles seem to pass away while in the midst of a cloud-like mire. Everything may seem like too much bother. This break from the world of doing into the world of being may seem like a step backwards, but is often a step toward healing.

As everything else is falling away, we need that time-out from life's busy-ness to re-group, prioritize, and put things in a new order. We need time to process our emotions and incorporate the changes grief brings into our lives.

One often emerges from a depression with a new burst of energy and a new direction and a different perspective of the world. For me, a sign that I'm ready to make a major change is to begin to clean out my closets. It's a Herculean task that is never-ending. I accumulate more stuff than anyone I know! It all seems so needed, but boxes and boxes go to the Thrift Shop each year and there's still more. I wonder what possessed me to buy all that stuff in the first place! Actually I've just undergone a change of my perception of things. What once seemed to fulfill a need or a want now no longer does, and should be discarded. How often do we hold on to pieces of ourselves that should be discarded?

Depression is a type of meditation. It draws one into oneself. It shuts out the world outside and focuses in on the world inside. If ever one can hear the voice of God it is in the special place, beyond prayer, deep within the quiet still point of one's soul.

If we change our perception of depression and view it as healing and meditative, we take away the stigma of guilt and uselessness that is often attached to depression. That frees one to benefit from some of the healing qualities of this self-imposed time-out.

King David certainly suffered with deep depression. One can read it in many of his psalms. Jesus agonized in the garden of Gethsemane. In fact, the word used to describe the experience was *agonia* (Greek), from which the word *agony* is derived—certainly a good way to describe the grieving process. Jacob grieved nearly unto death because of the loss of his son Joseph . We are in good company as we grieve.

In the Bible, depression often precedes a major event or change in life—almost as if it was a needed respite to rally one's forces before attacking, or beginning again. Depression is a hollowed-out space;

when filled it can become a lake of creation. Prayer is a way to share grief, even when one feels completely alone. I'm reminded of this often-told story:

> One night a man had a dream. He dreamed he was walking along the beach with the Lord. Across the sky flashed scenes from his life. For each scene, he noticed two sets of footprints in the sand—one belonging to himself, and the other belonging to the Lord. When the last scene of his life flashed before him, he looked back at the footprints in the sand. He noticed that many times along the path of his life there was only one set of footprints. He also noticed that it happened at the very lowest and saddest times in his life. This really bothered him and he questioned the Lord about it. "Lord, you said that once I decided to follow you, you would walk with me all the way. But I have noticed that during the most troublesome times in my life, there is only one set of footprints. I don't understand why, when I needed you most, you would leave me." The Lord replied, "My son, my precious child, I love you and I would never leave

you. During your times of trial and suffering, when you see only one set of footprints, it was then that I carried you."

Often when we feel completely alone there are unseen hands to sustain us.

❦

I'm sitting in a hospital room watching Kathleen in the dying process. She has stopped eating and now wants almost no liquids of any kind. Her body is shutting down and she is between two worlds: half-lucid, half-dreaming. I'm always amazed at the calmness surrounding the dying person. Modern medicine has allowed for a near-painless experience. Mostly, Kathleen needs reassurances. I hold her hand and tell her it is all right. She cries out that she's falling and I assure her that she is okay and that I am here. I never met Kathleen before, but she instantly trusts me and I feel completely connected to her. I smile often and touch her in the most soothing, motherly ways that I can think of. She tells me often that she's afraid. I tell her not to be.

We used to be there with the dying. Huge cradles

were built to help the sick and dying in Colonial times. They were rocked and made to feel secure. Our pain killers are truly remarkable, but where is the comforting?

I wish our hospitals had more soothing gentle music playing, instead of the blare of television. Of course, the sound of human voices can be comforting to some. Hospitals are rather noisy places: nurses, orderlies and doctors all doing their various work, while people come and visit and leave again. Even the night isn't silent. Medicines are given and patients checked on. Night lighting even keeps darkness at bay.

For me, a hospital, no matter how hard it tries, is not a place for great healings. Yet so few of us want the messiness of death, or the memories of a loved one dying in our homes. So hospitals have become places where one either recovers quickly, or goes to die. Hospice is a great organization to help with the process of dying. They try to hear the needs of the person dying as well as of the family and caregiver. I like their philosophy and support of the naturalness of death.

Comforting can take place on many levels. Fear and worry can be part of the dying process, but really there is absolutely no reason why the dying should worry. Sending love to the person to ease their mind as often as possible, holding the dying person's hand, smiling at them and stroking their face gently, help greatly. I do feel music helps to ease the soul. I always bring a Walkman with various tapes when I visit the dying.

Important new work is being done with music as a source of healing. Music can lower blood pressure and baseline metabolic rate and decrease respiration rate. Music can decrease the need for pain medications and anesthesia. It can stimulate the release of endorphins and salivary immunoglobulins (proteins capable of acting like antibodies which fight infection). Music has been used with premature babies with wonderful results. Hospitals are even experimenting with using live music in the operating room!

Live music works best because of the vibrations of the sound waves in the room. Don't worry if you can't play a note. Think of how comforting a mother's lullaby is. Softly singing or humming a lullaby is an instant relief, and you don't have to be a Pavarotti!

It is a curious fact that science catches up with our philosophy and general wisdoms. Many of the old folk remedies and herbal medicines are still important today. They work even if science hasn't figured out why. Chicken soup *does* make you feel better when you have a cold.

Conversely, some scientific truths make our own philosophies and beliefs clearer. Because of satellite communications, we can understand that a beam of light energy can be transmitted from space right into our own living rooms and that invisible radio waves can bring music and news of world events anywhere at anytime. Just one hundred years ago this would be science fiction along with the possibility of a man walking on the moon.

As our knowledge of outer space changes, so will our beliefs in the system of the universe and our role in the scheme of things.

> "There are more things in heaven and earth, Horatio, than are dreamt of in your philosophy."
> —Shakespeare, *Hamlet*

Health, aging, and the dying process are still untapped vistas. We truly know so little about them. As our knowledge expands, our whole way of viewing life will change also. We are constantly evolving.

CHAPTER 2

Grief and the Grieving Process

"What soap is to the body, tears are to the soul."
—Leo Rosten, from *The Joys of Yiddish*

Grief is the tearing asunder of your life. You are wounded and ruptured, and the pain you feel is both physical and emotional. You ache unto your very bones. Your heart literally aches as you spiral down into a world of confused feelings. This is the bottomless pit where both day and night meet in a twilight of suffering. While you may feel there is no undulating in this suffering, there are actually several stages to the process of grief. They fluctuate from passive to active phases, then back again in a see-saw of emotions.

Denial

Denial is a very powerful force. I have seen trained nurses deny the coming of death in a loved one, even though it was obvious to the most casual observer.

This very first reaction to a death often shows itself as shock, numbness or even disbelief. It feels so horrible to be without that special person in your life that you involuntarily shut down. Your mind becomes clouded. You can't think straight and can't seem to make even the simplest decisions. Perhaps you can't seem to care about anything or anyone at all. This feeling of shock acts as a blanket to numb the raw wounds. As a mourner, you are caught between two worlds. You have come face to face with the place where life and death meet and part. This view into death makes you vitally aware of your own mortality and the mortality of the whole living world.

With the death of a partner in a long marriage or relationship, you begin the process of uncoupling. Where two have been, there is now only one. You feel naked without your other half and each tiny step in life now feels new. You don't know to whom to turn, with whom to share, or how to be one on your own again.

Seeking to escape, your thoughts will travel back to an earlier time when you first met, courted and then married. You'll remember your life together as a series of pictures or events that flash before your eyes. This is a time of necessary regression. You cannot look forward yet, so you look back. This brings some respite from the pain and a comfort from the loss.

It is a time to bring out old love letters and cards, wedding pictures and family video tapes, even that special music that meant so much to you. It is a time for quiet contemplation. Tears may or may not flow, but the feeling of unreality is nearly impossible to shake off. You will be eased by remembering the past.

If you have lost a child, this devastating grief may be made even more difficult by you and your spouse having different mourning needs and different ways of grieving. You may wish to help each other, only to find that you cannot. There may be anger and blame to be resolved and the pain of the loss can become a wall between you. It is not that you are sharing the same grief; each of you has your own unique grief that is yours alone. You both may need help to scale the wall that divides you. Honestly sharing your feelings is the only way to share the grief that you are each experiencing. But sometimes words, even sounds, are just impossible. Try non-verbal communication through movement. Hold hands, embrace each other, rock together, cry together, moan together. Give your partner a back and shoulder rub and a neck massage. Hold your partner as you both gently rock back and forth. There is great comfort in the act of rocking together.

If you need help to get you through, this is a natural part of the gift of grieving. Reach out to friends, your community, your spiritual minister, rabbi or priest, church or synagogue, or professional consultants.

Ultimately grieving is a growing process where you learn your depths and limits and possibilities. It is a journey of change.

∾

Tears

The wellspring of our pain is released in tears. I thank God for the blessings of tears. They connect us to our mothers and foremothers, sisters, brothers, fathers and children. Tears express what words cannot and they connect generation to generation.

Tears are a blessing, a true gift from God. They open to the pain in the core of our souls. Tears are the liquid release that carry us through the darkest part of our mourning. Tears are a natural cleanser, a blessing that starts moving the pain outward. This blessing of tears is open to everyone.

Tears are often our first step out of the numbness of denial. Tears may feel stagnant but they are not. Tears are actively cleansing, yet they stop the normal hurriedness of an active life.

Beyond denial, and under anger, is pain: the pain of loss, the pain of death, and the pain of complete separation. We are desolate and alone. Tears open us up to the feelings within. They express our fears, anguish, desolation and our utter frustrations. We may howl at the moon. We may rage at the darkness and emptiness, but tears sweep over us, washing us anew.

Tears connect us to our humanness. We may feel alone while crying, but tears connect us to each other, to the tradition of our ancestors, to our progeny and to all humanity. This connection is powerful, a strong current of feeling conducted by the medium of our own tears.

Anger

After the passive, numbing unreality of the initial reaction to death, the mourner re-enters into an active stage of mourning. Anger and anxiety rule this stage as the mourner slowly realizes the full impact of the death on his or her real time-life.

Death always leaves a vacancy and a chaotic disorder. Legal papers, insurances, medical and funeral expenses and arrangements, cleaning out the private papers as well as the clothes closets—all feel like overwhelming chores. Why did this person die and leave me alone with all these problems? Panic sets in as the transforming quality of mourning shifts to its active stage. One feels the pressure of this death colliding with the pressures of life. Anger is the most natural expression of this inner turmoil. One feels this overwhelming anger toward the dead person. A diatribe of: "If only you'd listened to me, the family, your doctors," etc. or "Why didn't you take all precautions to prevent this death? Why didn't you eat right? See your doctor? Exercise regularly? Research alternative health methods or develop a more spiritual path?" In fact, this anger breaks through the bonds of numbness and tears and is often the first step in recovery. This anger is not restricted to the deceased alone. You may feel equally angry toward the world. "Why didn't they find a cure for this dreadful disease by now?"

In fact, most of the anger can be summed up in one word, WHY? "Why me? Why now? Why them?" You feel at odds with the world over this death.

How can this anger be helpful to you on this journey? First of all, remember that anger is part of the healing. You are examining the dark side of your own life as well as the dark side of death. Look well into it, for it will reveal many things that you didn't want to see during your loved one's life. It will also reveal things about the core of your fears and that can make for greater progress later.

Suicide is more complex. One goes through all the other steps of grieving, but with an added concern: suicide involves choice. When you mourn for a suicide you must come to grips with the fact that this person chose death over life. There is no hiding from this fact and anger and guilt often revolve around this issue of choice.

Don't try to repress the rage, but do channel it in some appropriate way. If you need physical release for your anger, choose carefully so that you don't harm yourself or others. Physical exercise is a great release, especially swimming. Being submerged in a pool is very nurturing for the body. Just walking along a beach, the rhythm of the waves begins to affect my breathing. A punching bag or padded combat sticks can also be an effective tool. Working out in a gym or power walking with clenched fists can help to relieve the anger.

Some people find screaming a great release, but I don't. The vibrations of the scream can be very detrimental in a home. If screaming feels right, go for scream therapy at some appointed place. Do it out in the country with no one around. Or scream under the roar of a passing train, where no one else will be disturbed by your anger. Screaming sets up highly energized vibrations which can be harmful or frightening to others. Screaming in an enclosed room can cause problems, because the vibrational energy remains there for a long period of time. So be warned and be careful about screaming.

There is silent screaming. Although not voiced, the energized vibrations emanate from the body from sheer intent. Walk into a room filled with angry people and you'll feel it, even though no one has said a word. Silent screaming should be voiced through chanting, singing, or simply opening your mouth and saying "EEEEE" for as long as your breath holds out and repeating that several times. Try it! It really does work. The "EEEE" sound engages the throat muscles and the jaw is in a clenched position. This creates a great release for tension and doesn't have the negative side effects of screaming.

Singing or chanting are also excellent ways of releasing body tensions and anger. Playing a musical instrument can soothe, or energize, while releasing tensions. Remember, it's music that soothes the savage breast!

Anger is an active step on this journey of transition, but look under the anger and you will often find hurt. It is difficult to recognize the hurt beneath the anger. Somehow it feels easier to be angry than to be caught in the painful hurting.

Guilt

Guilt is the phase of grief that personalizes the loss to you and you alone. It is your own particular place in this loss. If anger can be summed up in the word WHY, then guilt can be summed up in the word IF. If only I had been different, felt differently, acted differently, perhaps this wouldn't have happened. This guilt is part of the fantasy that one can control the destiny of another. This is a myth, but a potent one. Blaming oneself for a loss in one's life is universal. Rationally you may know that it isn't your fault, but as you relive your life, you can see all sorts of ways, in hindsight, to have avoided that place where you are now grieving.

We all would like to think that we have some magic power that could keep death at bay, but we do not. Accidents happen, crimes happen, illnesses happen, and neither do we control this world, nor each other. Tragedy happens, loss happens. Sartre wrote that we are our choices. The sum total of our lives is made up of the daily choices we have chosen to make. Guilt is the result of dealing with the outcomes of our choices in the most personal, private way. When Cain asked,"Am I my brother's keeper?" he was exploring the question of guilt in a relationship.

The only way to relieve this guilt is to forgive yourself. No one else can do this for you. You must come to peace with this loss.

Journal writing is an effective tool during the entire journey of loss. It's a way to crystallize your thoughts, especially when the feelings themselves may be difficult to define. Journal writing can take several forms: diary entries, poetry, letters, notebook journal or dictation on tape. Creativity in any form is a great release in channeling of emotional energies. For many artists, their grief has become channeled into great music, art, sculpture, novels, poetry, dance and even inspiration in other fields. The grief process can produce remarkable results.

Guilt is an all-pervasive feeling that can mix with anger, depression, denial and even acceptance. The feeling of guilt may come and go throughout all the stages of this process.

Depression

Feeling the hurt is a passive phase of the mourning process. After all the anger, one needs the respite of this stage. The mourner usually experiences this as a deep and prolonged depression. This is no longer the shock of early denial, but the true realization that life has indeed gone on without the loved one and all that this entails. This depression is painful, truly the dark night of the soul. Within this deeply painful place is a true seed for new growth, but the price one must pay is to look through the mirror darkly and see the changes this death has brought forth in you.

Psalm twenty-two is particularly meaningful to many in this phase of mourning.

My God, My God, why hast thou forsaken me?
Why art thou so far from helping me,

> *and from the words of my roaring?*
> *O my God, I cry in the daytime, but thou hearest not;*
>   *and in the night season, and am not silent. . . .*
> *I am poured out like water, and all my bones are out of joint:*
>   *my heart is like wax; it is melted in the midst of my bowels.*
> *My strength is dried up like a potsherd;*
>   *and my tongue cleaveth to my jaws;*
>   *and thou hast brought me into the dust of death.*

I can relate so strongly to these passages. Although written by David so long ago, the feeling of utter despair is still so palpable. Grief is the tearing apart of one soul from another, and this often means a re-evaluation of all other things in one's life, especially one's belief system. If David could wonder if God had forsaken him, then it is natural to wonder about one's connection with God during the grieving. Some may find it impossible to pray to God at this time; others may immerse themselves totally in prayer. The grief process tests one's belief system no matter how firmly rooted it has been in the past. One needs to find the courage to delve unafraid into the thoughts, feelings and beliefs that emerge at this time. Great growth is only possible with utter and complete honesty. The time for fooling oneself has passed and the true work of healing has begun.

I envision this part of grieving as healing the wound. One has found the sore place, the gaping wound, the hurt and sorrow. Now one begins the painful job of binding the wound. As with all wounds this place must be cleansed thoroughly with honest evaluation and soul-searching or else festering will ensue. Once cleansed and closed the true job of healing can begin.

This is often the most difficult part of the process, but bear in mind the old adage that it is always darkest before dawn. I am reminded of the story of a great and powerful king who could find no joy in his court, his kingdom or his life. This king became melancholy and depressed. Finally in desperation he decreed that whoever could cheer him would be rewarded with his weight in gold. A myriad of clowns, magicians, comedians, minstrels and actors appeared before the king seeking that prize of gold, only to be disappointed. Nothing seemed to remove the heavy weight of melancholy from the king's shoulders.

One day a quiet young scholar entered the court. He had been studying with a great and wise master and although of tender years, he possessed a quality of peace and contentment about him. He approached the king and told him simply to remember but one thing: THIS, TOO, SHALL PASS. The king astonished his court by breaking into a smile. The irony of it! All that this great king would do, all that this great king would have, all that he and his court would accomplish in their lives—all this, too, shall pass.

All the king's worries, pain, melancholy, depression, sorrow: this, too, shall pass. The king felt a great weight lift and his spirit rejoiced as he repeated, "This, too, shall pass!" Then the king ordered, "Pay this man his weight in gold!" And so it was done.

A year passed happily in the kingdom. The king returned diligently to the duties of his land. The court delighted in their sovereign's new-found contentment and happiness. One day the king ordered the young scholar back into his council room and told him that although he had been extremely happy, he suddenly realized that *this*, too, would pass. The king feared this would come true and that he would again fall into a dark melancholy. He asked the scholar his advice, and the scholar said simply, "Such is the way of the world."

The king had a ring made with the motto: THIS,

TOO, SHALL PASS, which he wore every day. On the archway to his castle, he had his artisans carve: SUCH IS THE WAY OF THE WORLD. And the king grew wise and never forgot what the young scholar had taught him.

Remember: loss is the ongoing process of change. In our grief we forget where we are on this path of life. We forget that this, too, shall pass and such is the way of the world. Simple lessons fit for a king.

Fear

The conquering of our fears is a lifelong task. Underlying *all* the stages in grief is fear: fear of change, fear of the unknown, fear of pain, fear of new beginnings, fear of inertia, fear of one's emotions, fear of both life and death itself. Fear is such an all-pervasive emotion and not limited to loss or grief in particular, but part of the act of living and part of the general human condition.

I believe one cannot ignore fear and its potent impact on life. Many choices are made out of our fears. The greatest opportunity that loss gives us is a chance to face our fears and conquer them—easy words, but a very difficult task.

Acceptance

The challenge of the final stage of grief is to emerge from this deep soul-searching night and to actively *choose* life. It is necessary to *choose* life again after grief. This is much more difficult than it first sounds. Before you can choose life you must come to the realization that the previous part of your life is truly over. All your wishing it back will be to no avail and it is time for closure.

Most people have the hardest time with this stage of grief. After all, one can get used to almost anything and by now grief has been a close companion for a long while. One has become accustomed to the feelings surrounding mourning. The act of mourning itself continues to connect you with your loved one.

Some may find it nearly impossible to begin the process of closure. I believe it is often due to the guilt they feel that they are still alive. Often the guilt hits hardest just when they are venturing out again, just when enjoying a dinner out with friends, or when ready to start a new relationship. In other words, just when we are ready to choose life again, we pull back into grief with guilt.

It's time to let go of the past, knowing it's always

a part of you and that it's always available through memories. But now it is time to move on. How to get over that big step? First, begin the work of closure. Say goodbye to your loved one in a new way, without pulling them back toward you. Share your thoughts that life is still exciting to you and thank your loved one for all the joy that you shared. Acknowledge that their death has led you to this new place and although you wish they were with you now, they aren't. Acknowledge that they are in a new place, too, and adjustments are being made by both of you.

You are moving forward with a new knowledge of yourself, your life and your beliefs. It is time to begin to share that with the world. It is time to emerge from your mourning. You are now that butterfly ready to take flight into the morning of a new day.

CHAPTER 3

The Healing Process

"Death is neither a decree nor a punishment but is a part of creation."

—KENNETH KRAMER

IN THIS CHAPTER we will deal with both myths and realities surrounding grieving. Let's begin by dispelling some of the major myths about grief.

MYTHS

- **MYTH: Grief can be shared.** This process of growth is unique to each person. One can share similarities in this experience with others, which is why bereavement groups offer a great aid to recovery. Nevertheless, your mourning process remains your own. You will move through it at your own pace. How else could you experience the growth and change that mourning will ultimately bring you?
- **MYTH: After you've gone through one

stage, you've passed it forever. Wrong—you'll come and go through anger into pain and back to depression, only to find yourself with anger again. There may even be times that denial returns, when you can almost see your loved one coming through the door. The stages of grief are not like rungs of a ladder, each one above the other. They are more like tides in the ocean, coming and going in waves.

Guilt and fear are two handmaidens that will come and go throughout mourning. In fact, conquering fear is one of the great lessons in life. We all need to conquer our fears in order to progress to the next steps. Although fear itself is a universal emotion, each person has his own perceived fears and ways of dealing with them. Timing is most important. When we are *ready* to deal with the fear, it will be a much easier process to move through. Waiting for our own timing is difficult and frustrating. Many of us want to lunge forward without any preparation and dive right into it. Others are so timid that no amount of preparedness feels like it is enough. It is a delicate balance. Waiting for your own timing will aid your ability to face your fears more effectively.

- **MYTH: We grieve only when there is a death.** We grieve loss, not death. A person can go through a grieving process over the loss of one's hair, the loss of one's childhood, the loss of one's home or possessions. **Any loss whatsoever can bring on grieving.** The causes can range from rape to losing a job, with a myriad of subjects in between. It doesn't matter what is the cause, the common thread in loss is *change*. The more dramatic the change feels to you, the greater the chance that you will need time to grieve over that loss.

- **MYTH: Family and friends will always be there when we need them, especially when we are in mourning.** I wish it were true that we could depend on others to be there for us, because we are most vulnerable during this time. Unfortunately something I call the Judas factor occurs. Someone in your close circle of friends or family will not be able to deal with either the loss or the process of mourning. Usually that person feels so uncomfortable or embarrassed or afraid and unsure that they cannot come forward to help you. You, in the midst of your grief, will feel betrayed and this will cause you more deep pain. It's sort of a double whammy. It's like being kicked in the stomach when you're down on the ground. The closer the friend the more it will devastate you. It is never a situation for which we can ever feel prepared.

Society is partially to blame for this phenomena, since death is not an integrated part of our lives in the Western world as it is in the East. In oriental cultures, children are raised in a very mannered and structured way in society. They are taught what is expected of mourner, family and friends. Our rituals regarding death are hidden from our general society and we tend to live with little regard to manners or customs. We live in a false antiseptic vision of the world where death has no place and is considered an embarrassment. Most of us know little of our own religious customs surrounding death and mourning and positively nothing of the customs in other faiths and cultures. Knowledge is power and knowing what is expected and how to act will ease the awkwardness.

The awful realization of the Judas factor is

often balanced with what I call the angel factor. This is when someone from out of the blue will help you, give you advice, or soothe you just when you need it most. It could be an acquaintance, someone you've lost touch with or even a stranger you've just met. Age doesn't matter. The advice can come from a young child, a very elderly person or literally anyone. It will seem as if an angel is by your shoulder whispering hope and helping to dispel fears. This helps to balance the devastation from the Judas factor. Often one finds a new understanding and sometimes a new friend.

- **MYTH: Phases come one by one, in orderly sequence.** As if this process weren't hard enough, feelings of loneliness, despair, panic, anger, guilt, shame and sorrow often overlap. In fact, you could feel all the above emotions at once. This makes the sorting of your emotional roller coaster most trying. Many times the act of grieving brings up old unresolved issues that may have nothing directly to do with the loss, but which were triggered by it. That presents a triple whammy!

- MYTH: **Time alone heals.** Unresolved issues can get buried with time, but they are still there and fully powerful. I have watched two sisters fighting over which one their mother favored with such vehemence, even though they were both in their eighties and their mother had died over forty years ago! It didn't matter. The hurt and pain and jealousy were as real now as when the slighting occurred. Sometimes we gain insight and wisdom with age and time, but old issues need to be released of their power to hurt. And old issues often surface after a death.

Focusing on things in the past promotes the illusion that time stands still. One can get frozen in reworking a past that cannot be changed. This becomes a defense which can keep one from facing the present.

Sometimes it feels more comfortable to try to curl up into the past, especially when the present is so difficult. We all know people who try to do this by building a shrine to the loss. People who never change the room of their loved one, or make even the slightest changes in their lives. Journal writing of daily thoughts and emotions can help to clarify shifting moods and frustrations. It can also lead to a clearer picture of one's growth and change in the future.

A new twist on journal writing and support groups for those with access to computers with on-line services, such as Internet, is the whole world of the "information highway." There is even SeniorNet, with access to many kinds of help with grief and bereavement. This is a lifesaver at two o'clock in the morning when you need somebody to talk with. You don't even need to get dressed. There is no guilt about disturbing your family and there is a comfortable feeling about the rhythms of typing. You might meet a friend indeed in cyberspace. Isn't technology wonderful?

SHAME

Shame is a discomfort we feel about our own vulnerability. We are embarrassed by our wounds. Our loneliness, pain, confusion, anger, tears and inability to cope are humiliating. We feel naked and alone, caught in some unspeakable act—the act of great sorrow. To compound this there is an old superstition that somehow death is communicable. People give you a wide berth if they think you are dying or that you are in great sorrow. It brings death too near to their lives. This often makes people too uncomfortable. Faced with their own issues around loss and death, they feel embarrassed and ashamed. It is just so much easier to avoid the mourner rather than to deal with their own feelings and fears. This may explain why the Judas factor exists in the grief process.

Unresolved Issues

Death often brings up unfinished business. Old jealousies and disputes that were never fully resolved resurface after a death. Many times families pull apart rather than come together. Don't be fooled by the claim that money and possessions seem to be the divisive issues; that just covers up the feelings of anger, pain and loss. We invest material things with power. A promised ring may indeed bring you comfort, but you may feel a double loss if that ring goes to your "hated" cousin. The ring is really not the issue; it is the anger that you feel over this double loss. Sometimes what is, is not fair! Still you must deal with what you cannot change. Charles Dickens' *Bleak House* is about squabbling heirs to a huge fortune that is completely gone due to the long court process. Sometimes even the winner can be the loser. No one said that this would be easy.

Death often leaves unfinished business that haunts us during the mourning period. Rage and pain and sorrow may only express our feeling of lost opportunities. Life goes on and yet one needs to have a sense of closure and completion. Having some type of ceremony or ritual can help bring a sense of closure. Symbolically we can address our loved one and our loss. Dealing with other unresolved issues that the grieving process may bring to the surface can be difficult without some type of psychotherapy.

Remember, you may need help to get through this grief. Your body will be stressed and you may become physically ill. Try to watch your diet and eat nutritious meals. Consult with your physician, especially if depression or illness become problems. Don't be afraid to seek help from therapists, doctors, self-help groups and spiritual ministers. This is not an easy time for anyone. The body is being stressed mentally, spiritually, emotionally and physically. Be kind to yourself. Make sure you are getting all the help you need. Don't be ashamed of this natural process that you are going through. It is a great gift to receive help when you truly need it.

Living in a small New England village for the last several years has been both a blessing and a lesson for me. The blessing has been in the many wonderful people it has been my privilege to know, one of whom was Lillian.

Lillian looked like a human question mark from her crippling arthritis. I often wondered how she managed to see to cross the street. Every day she rose before five o'clock in the morning to stoke the kitchen wood-fired stove. She and her sister lived alone in a large white Victorian house, and never did any stray animal lack for a meal if it came by. Their kindness to all animals was phenomenal: cats, dogs, birds were all lovingly fed, often before the sisters themselves. But I'm straying from my point. Lillian had a rather simple mind that became easily confused, but she felt strongly that within the village everyone should know each other. She decided that whoever she saw must be introduced to anyone else who happened to be around. Her favorite place to do this was outside the village post office. Unfortunately Lillian often got the whole thing hopelessly muddled. She would get everyone's name wrong as well as where they came from, what they did or where they were living. This often caused some embarrassment for all, as we quickly corrected every single word out of Lillian's mouth. No matter, the result was an introduction that perhaps would not have happened if not for Lillian. Dear Lillian "rushed in where angels fear to tread," and she was smart enough to risk being herself. It little mattered to her about formalities, or what others thought. Her intent was that village people should know each other and this she accomplished.

I myself tend to shy away from introducing myself and realize the courage it took to not care what others might think. I am about to take that leap of courage straight from Lillian's example and hope the intent comes through without all the muddle.

One short aside about Lillian. When she was dying, the neighborhood kept vigil. Someone sat at her hospital bed day and night for nearly a week. At her funeral we all knew that the village was marking the passing of a very special light, the like of which we will not see again.

TOUCHING

Human beings need to be touched. I do not mean this lightly, symbolically, or flippantly. I mean this quite literally! It is a physical human need that knows no age. Premature babies grow when gently massaged daily. They develop more quickly and with fewer problems. We thrive on touch and don't know it.

After the world wars there were many orphaned babies. New hospitals were built to house the babies—all sterile, white, sanitary—but they found an extremely high death rate there. Babies were fed by automatic bottle-holders with little nurse contact. Many babies curled up in the fetal position. They shriveled up, refused to eat, seemed to age and wrinkle, then died. After looking into this phenomenon it was found that one orphanage had no deaths at all. It was an older building but there was lots of visual stimulation, and the nurses held and fed each baby several times during the day. We need human contact; no feeding machine can replace touching.

Somehow we forget this with the elderly who often live alone with little human interaction, let alone human touch. We need to be touched to maintain health. The energies around the body become atrophied and a glass-like crystal surrounds them. Energies become trapped inside, making exchange difficult. Touch shatters that crystal allowing an opening of free-flowing energy. I encourage you, when visiting elderly people, to hold their hands, stroke their back and give lots of hugs. This exchange is not only good for the soul, it's good for the body.

When you are in deep sorrow, your energies become stuck around you without that free and open interchange. Use a loofah or washcloth to stroke your body, especially the underside of your arms. Consciously, using long strokes, brush down your body from head to toe. If you can afford to, go to a licensed massage therapist.

The body can hold memories in the muscles. Massage not only moves the energies around the body, but it can also trigger a memory release. This is experienced as a flash picture while a certain muscle in the body is being worked on.

Therapeutic massage may be a bit painful in places. You may also feel a bit nervous or awkward. Just simply talk to the therapist. There is no need to do anything that you feel uncomfortable about; this is not about sexual stimulation. You may find massage a difficult venue if you have experienced any abuse in the past. In that case, learn some simple self-massage techniques. There are many books on the market that can help you. If this is a new experience, view it as an adventure and just try to relax into the experience. I'm a strong believer in massage. In Scandinavian and Oriental cultures, massage is a part of routine health maintenance.

The concept of energies moving in and out of the body is not a new one. The chakra system, important in Indian culture, corresponds to the spine and head with seven vortexes of swirling energy centers. There are many books that explain the chakra system.

The Chinese speak of the life force as Chi which moves along meridian lines and through specific pressure points along the body. Acupuncture is the ancient method of healing by stimulating specific points to release energies in the body. T'ai Chi is a way of using the total body to release energy through movement. Yoga also releases energy in a similar way. Holding different yoga positions changes the breath as well as heart rate. The various combinations of holding and moving can release tension as well as energies.

Western science is just now catching up with these methods and ideas. In China and Japan, T'ai Chi is seen as a way of life, and the elderly remain relatively mobile and healthy into old age. In India many Yogic masters have the vim and vitality of people half their age. I'm sure that diet and nutrition play equal parts in their health. Not being an expert in medicine or nutrition, I suggest reading Deepak Chopra's books as a source for information.

TAKING CONTROL

It is a proven fact that the mind controls the body. In changing your thoughts, your brain will release different chemicals into the bloodstream. Think happy thoughts and your body, through your brain, responds in positive and healing ways. The opposite is also true. Unhappy thoughts result in negative physical responses that can often lead to illness. Unfortunately, in mourning it is seldom easy to think happy thoughts. Your challenge is to change your thought patterns.

One of the easiest ways to do this is to change your breathing patterns.

Breathing Excercise 1

Take a deep breath into your belly and sigh it out. Repeat that three times and you will feel different: probably more relaxed, maybe even calmer.

Breathing Excercise 2

Now try the same exercise but start by standing straight and on the inhalation raise your arms, palms facing the ceiling, to the overhead position. Now hold your breath in and count to eight with your arms reaching for the sky! As you sigh the breath out, turn your hands palms down and slowly lower them to your sides. Do this three times and feel the difference between the two exercises. The first one you can do anywhere at all. It is a simple and effective tool in releasing tension.

Let's talk a bit about emotions. The body receives emotions as electric impulses that generally come through the senses to the brain which transmits these energies through the body. The brain itself can trigger these energies to release chemicals into the blood, increase heart rate, etc., and all it needs is your thoughts. We have all experienced this. You suddenly remember that you left your wallet in the car or your pocketbook at the restaurant. You instantly panic and the brain sends the emotional messages through electrical impulses for you to react. Your breathing may quicken, your heart rate increase, you may even break out into a sweat or feel queasy in your stomach. All because of an emotion (panic) that was triggered by thought (electrical impulses). Suppose that you find your wallet was in your breast pocket, instead of the back pocket where you usually put it? While your mind and intellect may be immediately relieved, you still must deal with the reactions that your emotions have manifested in your body. The same thing happens with the emotions of grief and mourning. These emotions are transferred as electrical energies in the body.

The good news is that these energies can be moved through the body. Tears move energies. Breathing exercises, yoga, T'ai Chi, meditation, exercise and massage can all be used to release and move energies out of the body. You need to take responsibility for yourself. You have choices; now you must choose.

The greatest resistance to the work I do is that people don't want to take personal responsibility. They want someone else to do the work, someone else to make it all right, even if that someone is God. Of course friends, professionals, and yes, God, can certainly help; but you are the one with the free will to decide and the responsibility to do it.

Reb Zusia, a Hasidic master (Jewish 17th century movement in Poland) once said to his students:

"When God calls me, I will not be taken to account about why I was not a better Moses or a better Abraham. I will have to account for why I was not a better Zusia." We all need to meet that challenge. Being responsible for *our* choices, *our* life.

Knowing that energies can be moved through the body, you can choose, if you wish, to use that knowledge to ease your mourning process in whichever ways feel comfortable for you.

Personal Timing

Timing is an all-important part of life in general, and of grieving in particular. You cannot rush your own timing. There is no set pace, no set path for you to take. It is indeed a journey, and as in all journeys, you will learn new things along the way, practice and refine known skills and learn more about yourself by the end of the journey.

I always carry a journal with me on my travels. I enjoy reviewing the day and writing my impressions of the place where I am traveling. Mourning is a journey of discovery. If you can write about it in some way, you will find that it not only helps to clarify your thoughts, but also acts as a review and will be something to treasure later on in your life.

One of the points I have been trying to make in this chapter is that your perception of this experience can change the experience itself. Death is not a punishment and mourning can be viewed as a way to deal with loss. Transition is part of life itself. I cannot stress this enough. New things await you. Changes are happening in your body and your life. This is a period of transition, and hard as it may be, you will learn much from this process. I have often seen a complete new blossoming and turnabout after the grieving ends. Women start college or change professions, choosing to do what they have always wanted to do. Many women seem to come into their own after the death of their spouse. That is not to say that they weren't very happily married, but often a relationship calls for compromise. When on their own, they make all the decisions and are basically responsible for themselves. I use women as my example because it is a fact that women more often outlive men. Also in this society men seem to make fewer compromises about career choices. Men, after the death of their spouse, often remarry. They, too, are in transition and learn about nurturing and sustaining life without a female influence. That is quite a learning lesson.

When I speak of energies in and around the body,

and that emotions are part of the electric system in the brain, I know this may be difficult to understand. Words are defined by both connotation and denotation and so may mean slightly different things to different people. Such is the limitation of the written word. So let me give you an example of what I mean. Suppose you are in a darkened movie theater watching a very sad scene (like the shooting of Old Yeller) that touches a deep place in your heart. You know this is only a movie and that no one or no animal has really been hurt, yet you feel a great sadness growing in your throat. Your throat feels constricted and tight. We call that "having a lump in our throat." I call it energies that have collected in your throat chakra area. Now what I mean by moving those energies is that you can bring up the energies to release in tears and have a good cry in the theater. Or you can swallow this "lump" of energy/emotion and send it into your stomach. From there it will try to process downward, eventually moving to the low belly area. Ever had a stomachache after an emotional experience? Maybe even vomiting? One other option remains and that is to leave the energies in the throat area without releasing them. The restricted throat will make it difficult to talk or express yourself. This can last for quite a long while. Energies do eventually dissolve or move to a particular place and settle there. Settled energies can stay within the body indefinitely, often encapsulating and forming a shell or lump.

I can see the energies that form in the same way around a person's heart, or belly. When in deep mourning these energies often get stuck around all these areas, especially the heart. Moving the energies out of the body will make the mourning process easier.

Pets and Grief

Animals are such an important part of our lives that we often forget what a great service they do for us. Many studies have shown that bringing dogs or cats into a hospital or nursing home is extremely beneficial to the patients. Stroking a pet can lower blood pressure; it is calming and can even help relieve depression—so much so that many hospitals have an Adopt-A-Pet program to help patients with healing.

How can animals do this? Our pets communicate their needs and wants without speaking, yet seldom does a pet owner not understand what his particular animal wants. Animals can absorb the energies around them, through their senses, and interpret that information. I call this "energy-eating."

When you are in grief, your normal routine of doing things changes. Your own depression changes the chemicals in your body so that you give off a different odor, which your pet can detect. Crying fills the room with different energy vibrations just through the sound waves that crying creates. This, too, your pet can easily sense.

While you are going through this grief experience, so will your pets and your children and your family. Be especially sensitive to this. Spend extra time stroking your pet. Spend time taking walks or other special activities. Be aware that if a death will cause a vacancy in the pet's household, the animal will be missing that person, also, missing the person's presence and smell and warmth.

In essence, your pet is feeling the unexplained loss and is grieving, too. Let your pet sleep with some article of the missing person's clothing. The scent of the person will help in the adjustment. Also be aware that this is hard on your pet as well as yourself and that the stress may cause illness, or temporary loss of appetite or listlessness. Just as you may need to see a doctor, your pet may need to see a veterinarian who may prescribe vitamins or a change in diet.

I realize that it is hard to think of others while in the midst of deep grieving, but we are responsible for our animals as well as for other people in our lives. If you honestly cannot cope, then you must ask someone else to care for your pet during your grief.

Many times a pet has helped in moving the grief process along. Your pet is your friend and can help in this painful journey. So be kind to each other.

In our society mourners are invisible. No one goes around wearing black armbands. No wreath is placed on the door to identify a house of mourning. For all your pain, no one knows you are grieving. This was not always the case. In the ancient city of Jerusalem, there was a special path to the Temple that was used only by mourners. This identified them and gave them the comfort of knowing all the other mourners in the community. It also allowed them the special greeting by the other members of the community: "May God comfort you among the mourners of Zion and Jerusalem." This daily affirmation of comfort and comforting thoughts must have indeed helped during their year of mourning.

Now we are left to comfort ourselves. We must find some daily affirmation, some comfort in the world, some hope within our souls.

Children and Mourning

Children are specially sensitive to the energies around them, so they are particularly aware of loss and mourning. This includes children from the youngest infants to teenagers. The concept of death will be unclear to most children younger than eight years old. At about second grade children become very interested in death. It is often a time when they have experienced some death in the family, in the community, or a pet. They want to know all about it—all about the customs, the actual nuts and bolts of dying, and the concepts of what happens afterwards. Don't ignore their questions, even if you don't have any answers. Share your true feelings, your own doubts and convictions. Don't let embarrassment close this avenue. You can learn from each other. Children's questions are often so direct and fresh and clear that they will stimulate your own thoughts. This is all part of the life-long journey that you take as a family. Don't exclude your children from the process.

Parents often want to shield their children from the idea of death. But remember they can feel the loss, the sadness, the anger. They are confused. They feel the changes in you and they have fears. You need to answer their questions honestly.

Infants need special nurturing during this time. Baths are extra-soothing. Also soothing is holding a child or gently rocking it. Take the baby out into the fresh air. Young children should be given extra play time. Encourage them to move and skip and run. Let them draw and paint. Water play will be especially soothing. Fill a sink with warm water and detergent or bubble bath. Place metal or plastic measuring spoons and measuring cups in the water. Metal ones make nice noises when banged together. Use NO GLASS of any kind! Add sponges and any favorite bath toys. Also, letting young children hold their hands under warm running water is very calming and relaxing. This is a natural way of removing energies from the upper body.

Sharing your tears is a way to let your children know that crying is a natural part of life. This unconsciously gives them the permission to cry when they may need to do so without shame. Children learn best by example. They watch you and pick up more about you than you ever realize. Sharing your honest feelings will help them later on in life. This is a journey of discovery and recovery that you can share together on many different levels.

CHAPTER 4

A Time to Heal

*"For life and death are one,
even as the river and the sea are one."*

—KAHLIL GIBRAN

Now is the time to heal, and in healing a new and healthy part of you will emerge. One of the great tools for settling the mind and finding tranquility, even in the midst of chaos, is meditation. The Bible speaks of prayer and meditation going hand-in-hand. In prayer we rejoice, give thanks, ask forgiveness and request all sorts of aid. In meditation we still our minds to hear God's answers.

MEDITATION

Meditation is an ancient practice used by religious leaders, holy men and women, and mystics of many different faiths. It is prominent in the Judeo-Christian religions as well as in Buddhism and Hinduism. It is becoming increasingly popular in Western culture to use meditation as a technique for stress management. There are many fine books on how to meditate that are easily available to the public.

There are many different techniques, as well as breathing exercises, that can be used. Medical studies have shown that meditation slows the heart rate and lowers high blood pressure. It changes the blood chemistry in the body. It has also been linked with creativity. These are no mean feats for one simple practice. And it is a *practice*. Doing it one time might be relaxing, but it misses the whole point. You must practice meditation, make it part of your prayer time or part of your schedule. Making it part of your daily ritual in good times ensures that you can easily access that tranquil place during a crisis. This can only happen when meditation becomes natural and easy for you, in other words, when it is a comfortable habit.

Let's start with a simple technique.

1. Sit comfortably crossed-legged on the floor with a cushion, hands resting on the knees, palms facing upwards. Use a straight-backed chair without side arms, if this is easier for you.

2. Take a deep breath in through your nose and sigh it out of your mouth. Do this two more times.

3. On the third time, hold the breath in as long as you can. See what holding the breath does to your body. Where do you feel pressure? Where do you feel open? Where do you feel pain or tightness?

4. When you must, slowly release this breath and feel the lusciousness of that release.

5. Release all the breath that you can and hold the breath out for as long as possible. How does this feel different in your body? Where do you feel pressure? Where do you feel open? Where do you feel pain or tightness?

6. When you need to, take a large inhalation of air and resume normal breathing. See how this simple change in your breathing affects your whole body. I like to meditate with my eyes closed so that I can concentrate on the inner changes in my body. I also turn my telephone off so I won't be startled.

7. With the return to normal breathing, try to consciously empty your mind of thoughts and worries. I limit my meditation session to fifteen minutes. Setting a kitchen timer works wonderfully to keep you on the fifteen-minute schedule. Eventually, after many sessions, you will automatically know when the time is up.

I believe that everyone can benefit from just fifteen minutes without worrying. If I feel pressed by a particular worry or pressuring thought, I consciously say that I will think about it in fifteen minutes. It's a bit like Scarlett O'Hara saying, "I'll think about that tomorrow." I often find it amazing that worry may disappear not only for fifteen minutes, but for an hour, an afternoon or even a whole day. After all, tomorrow is another day!

Measured Breathing

When I find my mind being bombarded with thoughts—any thoughts at all—I begin a measured breathing.

1. Inhale to a slow count of four, then hold for a slow count of eight, then exhale for a slow count of four.

2. Repeat this several times, then resume normal breathing concentrating on the path of the breath as it goes in and out of the body.

3. If the count of four, eight, four doesn't work for you, try an inhalation to a count of eight, holding for a count of sixteen and exhaling a slow release of eight.

4. While truly concentrating on a measured-count of breathing, it is hard to have other thoughts. If you do, just release them and concentrate on your breathing. It doesn't matter if you feel a bit foolish or you aren't sure that you're getting it. Those are thoughts, so banish them!

5. After the fifteen minutes, stop.

6. Open you eyes, stretch out like a cat uncurling itself and resume your day. *If you need another session, do it later in the day.*

Find the time of day that works best for you and just do it. I like to use a darkened room, but sometimes it is glorious to meditate in a garden filled with sunlight. I often see bright swirling colors when I meditate. If you do, don't be afraid and just enjoy the light show. If you don't see anything, that's fine, too. Sometimes I've come out of meditation with a solution to a problem, or an answer to a question. I always come out of meditation more ready to face the day ahead with new and exciting possibilities and challenges.

There is no substitution for meditation. There are, as I said, various techniques. Search for one that suits you or use my simple technique with your own variations.

THE TRANSFORMING

"Suffering," in its original meaning, merely meant "undergoing." That explains, "Suffer the little children to come unto me." After all, how much suffering could it be to spend time with Jesus! Only in the original sense of undergoing can this make sense. We are all suffering and undergoing life and loss and grief and pain. How will grief and pain ever transform into joy?

To understand this transforming quality of grief, let's compare it to the digestive system. First, you "eat" grief; like food, it does enter into the body. You chew your food to break it into smaller pieces so that digestion can begin. In a similar way, anger acts like chewing to break apart the emotions into elements, or separate parts. You swallow and food may get stuck in your throat, just as feelings get stuck in that area. In the stomach, the acids work on breaking the food into nutrients. Grief gets broken through an inward process of reviewing the past and allowing the wisdom of time and perspective to carry you forward. If there is too much in the stomach, you may vomit. Grief can cause illness, too, as your body "throws up" the confusion of feelings that this change is causing. But there is nutrition in the grief. Needed elements for future growth are waiting to be absorbed into your life. This parallels the work of the small intestines on the now liquid food mixture. Eventually what cannot be absorbed, integrated and used is passed through the large intestines and out of the body. This is how a person uses food as the building blocks of the physical body. A potato must be broken down first in order to be absorbed as sugars for the body's use.

So, too, does grief get transformed into new growth helpful on the path of life. There is plenty of raw material; we just need to use it. Digestion takes time and so does transformation. You really can't rush it, or even skip a step. Imagine only swallowing food whole and what that would do to your digestive system! Each step is necessary for the next process forward.

ETHICAL WILLS

We have now become familiar with organ transplants and how a person can will different parts of the body to be used to give sight, and even life itself, to others. A person can will the physical heart, but what about what is inside that heart? What about the thoughts, lessons learned, loving feelings? How can these be passed on?

So much thought, arguments and strain are caused over the physical inheritance. Who will get the house, the cars, the property, the jewelry and all the money? But what about the real jewels of a person's life—all the lessons life has taught? How can these be passed down as a true inheritance for all in the family and even friends as well?

An Ethical Will is a document, audio or video tape that is designed to pass on wisdom, which is your spiritual wealth. The roots are well established in the Hebrew scriptures with Jacob's very moving parting words to each of his sons. In Deuteronomy, Jacob, now called Israel, speaks to each of his children, tells them their strengths and weaknesses, and speaks of the future he sees for them. Lying on his deathbed, Jacob advises each of the future tribes how to act, what to do and how to keep the spiritual path true to God.

There are many other examples from other periods in history. It was a common practice in medieval times for parents to write wills urging the specific moral or religious development for their children. This is the root of godparents for a child. Usually people placed in extreme situations where death is a definite possibility, such as soldiers of any era going off to war, or someone with a terminal illness, will create a letter (or videotape) to be opened at a specific time. Sometimes it is at a special occasion, like a wedding, or at some milestone marker, like a graduation. These Ethical Wills are extremely valuable to those receiving them and are treasured for a lifetime.

What if your loved one didn't leave an Ethical Will? You can write one in memory of that person. Think about what your loved one's life taught you. What special qualities do you miss? What acts of charity and kindnesses do you remember? What was important to your loved one? How has that person's life influenced you? What values did you share?

What would you like to keep and incorporate into your life now and in the future?

None of these are easy questions with one-word answers. Think about them and open to the inspiration around you. Do not be surprised if you feel the presence of your loved one near you as you think and work on what that person has given you that enriches life. You may find yourself dreaming special, meaningful and important dreams. You may find a deeper understanding of your own life. You may find yourself at true atonement—atonement meaning to be AT ONE WITH. The balance of peace with one's self and peace with the whole universe brings about true atonement. It is as simple as our own heartbeat, which is not heard by our own ears, but beats steadily all the same. Now we need to listen to the voice within.

For all of you who say, "Who am I that I should pass on my values?"—remember, you are the hero of your own life! No one but you could live your life, have your experiences, see the world through your eyes. Your life is a unique expression of all that you are and all that you have learned. I have never met a single person whose life didn't speak to me in some way. Your life lessons have value to others.

Creating Rituals

I come at last to closure with this reminder: **No one can do this mourning work but you!** You are responsible for your life choices even when you choose to do nothing. All the ideas and knowledge mean nothing if you refuse to try them or work through them. Too many people are waiting for someone else to rescue them.

I am reminded of a cartoon by Gaham Wilson of a blind skeleton holding a cup of pencils with a sign around his neck explaining his situation and asking for donations, while his bony finger is pressing the doorbell to the School for the Deaf. If the blind man had only walked on instead of waiting, so determinedly certain that help was about to answer his needs. We are all that blind man at some point in our lives.

Closure is a way of weaving the threads together. Emotionally we need an end to mourning and a way to continue on with life. We need to learn how to truly say good-bye without losing our past.

Ritual is a method of re-enacting emotions symbolically. This can be very helpful for closure in the grieving process. To create ritual you should first look to your religion's use of symbols. For example, the entire Mass is built around the symbols of unleavened bread (in Hebrew, *matzoh*) and wine as the re-enactment of a Passover seder meal. The power of the Mass shows the power that ritual can effect.

Each major religion has rituals for birth, death, burial and mourning. These act as ways to express deeper feelings and release the pain of the loss through the mysteries of religion. Start with these. They are familiar and will probably feel comfortable for you. If this is either not satisfying enough or not appropriate, then create a ritual for yourself.

First try to find something that's meaningful to you that you associate with the person who died. Did that person love the sun, have a bright sparkling smile, or did that person complain always about the cold? Then fire might be good to include. You could light a bonfire on a beach. Light an all-day candle. Use floating candles in a basin of water. Make little flat wooden boats, attach candles and float the lighted rafts on a lake at twilight.

Did the person love music? Then include a favorite song or go to a special concert. Sponsor a concert in memory of your loved one. Hire a musician to play at the graveside or for a memorial service.

Did the person love water? Rent a boat for a memorial service on water. Row a boat to the middle of a lake and pray. Buy a painting of the sea and hang it in a special place of honor.

Was the person very spiritual? Using the four elements of air, water, fire and earth in the ritual might be appropriate. Be creative. Air might be represented by balloons, wind chimes, burning incense or chanting. Water might be included simply by washing your hands, or sprinkling rose water (or holy water) or immersing in a ritual bath. Fire could be a votive candle, a bonfire on the beach or a Fourth of July sparkler. Earth could be a clay pot, a sculpture, a tree, flowers, or even a single smooth stone.

Use the symbols along with special prayers, poems, or music while holding hands and embracing. Be creative and even unique. If you have a special skill like dancing or juggling or playing the drums, perhaps these can be incorporated into the ritual. Think of how powerful it could be to have someone dancing, another person juggling and a third beating the rhythm on a drum.

One way to show continuation in a ritual is to recite the person's matrilineage and patrilineage for as far back as possible. For example: Karen, who is daughter of Margret and Paul, who is granddaughter of Esther and Sam, who is great granddaughter of Helen and Callum, etc. Then move the line forward into the future with her children, grandchildren and great grandchildren.

One could theoretically take one's lineage all the way back to Adam and Eve. It is a way to show that life continues and that we are all links in a chain of the family. One reason given for Adam (which in Hebrew means "of the earth") being our sole ancestor is to insure that we all understand that we come from the same source. We are all one family, genetically one species.

Creating ritual is not limited to closure work. You can decide to celebrate the birthday of the deceased in a special way. Or include a special Christmas present to the poor in their memory, or hang a special ornament on the tree as a way of including your loved one in your holiday times. You could light a candle on the anniversary of your beloved's death to acknowledge remembrance. Or plant a new rosebush each year. Or donate a flowering garden to your town park with a memorial plaque, or a special bench.

What you choose to create as ritual is infinite. It is personal and effective only if the intent is proper. Having the best and most meaningful closure will work only if, and when, you are ready to say good-bye. Otherwise, it is just a get-together. Again you must work within your own sense of timing.

CHILDREN AND RITUALS

Children especially need a ritual closure that they can participate in. Most adult symbols are too esoteric for children to feel a measure of closeness with. Children respond actively, so doing something, as well as explaining why this is being done, is important. For instance, a child could toss flower petals on a lake or river, or release a bunch of balloons (save at least one balloon for the child to keep), or be included in a circle of holding hands. The child should be told that this is a way of saying "good-bye" to the deceased. Ask the child if there is something special he or she would like to do to say "good-bye," and if at all possible include the child's wishes. Sometimes children come up with very healing ideas. Out of the mouths of babes....

I believe that death, like life, needs to be shared.

Rituals are a part of life that can give meaning to the more difficult parts. Children will experience grief both through you and on their own. Don't make it a lonely time for them. Include them in as much as both you and the child feel comfortable doing.

Change is both the most difficult and the most common lesson in life. Nothing stays exactly the same for even a second. Our cells keep moving, growing and dying. Our earth is in constant flux as it hurls in space. We are all a part of it, suffering it, "undergoing" it, participating in it. Loss is part of the ongoing change. Try to rejoice in your part of this great experience of life.

The year rolls 'round, cycling with its seasons and passages and rituals and holidays, and that is how we mark the days of our lives. Each day is for us to fill full of meaning and joy and wonder. How we do it is totally up to us. Many don't and are miserable. Many wait for another person to do the filling and they are the sad ones.

I encourage you to recognize the pattern of change in the consistency of everyday. Don't wait for perfection; we are all works in progress on this journey. Make life your own and each step of the journey will unfold for you. We are not alone. We are all part of "one big family hugging close to the ball of Earth for its life and being" (Carl Sandburg, *The Family of Man*). We are all part of the Universe. We are all part of life unfolding and evolving. Find your joy, even in the midst of suffering, and you will have a gift beyond gold.

> "Weeping may endure for a night,
> but joy cometh in the morning."
>
> —Psalm 30:5

CHAPTER 5

Transformation as Growth— Ways to Heal Yourself and Help Others

*"In the name of the Former, and of the Latter
And of their Holocaust. Allmen."*

—JAMES JOYCE

WE HAVE COME to the end of a journey, the end of one phase, or part. We are no longer "the Former" nor "the Latter," but a part of "Allmen." We have come through the "Holocaust" and have been transformed. We might look back and see our progress. Or perhaps like Jacob exclaim, "God was in this place and I knew it not." We will go on as different people because of this experience—with new awareness and hopefully more compassion for ourselves and others.

As a final way to show compassion and perhaps effect some healing, I would like to conclude this book with a list—not a complete list, by any means—a small list of ideas that you can do for yourself or others going through mourning. I know at times people just don't know what to do; that's the time to read over this chapter. Don't be afraid to modify or change or add to this list. I hope it will help you on this journey of transformation.

- Go for a walk.
- Bring a book of poetry to a park.
- Have a picnic.
- Invite a friend to share a picnic.
- Feed the ducks.
- Watch a sunset.
- Rise early and watch a sunrise. *(Do it right and make a thermos of tea/coffee and take a pretty mug to enjoy it in.)*
- Listen to classical radio.
- Read the psalms and think about how they speak to you in new ways.
- Call your friend. *(In all the research I did with people in mourning, this was the number one*

thing that helped them the most—having a friend call daily, or often.) ♥♥♥♥

- ♥ Invite someone to the movies.
- ♥ Read a great classic book that you always wanted to, but didn't get around to doing.
- ♥ Read a trash spy novel, romance or current best seller.
- ♥ Call or write an old friend that you haven't seen in years.
- ♥ Start a daily diary of your thoughts.
- ♥ Write a letter to your deceased beloved and put it away.
- ♥ Have your nails manicured—great for men as well as women.
- ♥ Go to a petting zoo and play with the animals.
- ♥ Play golf, tennis, racquetball, or whatever!
- ♥ Watch a sexy movie.
- ♥ Make some popcorn and share it with the birds.
- ♥ Make a special winter treat tree for the birds to feed on.

- ♥ Light candles with dinner.
- ♥ Take a bubble bath.
- ♥ Take a hot bath with a handful of fresh mint leaves or lemon slices floating in the water.
- ♥ Buy a new fragrant soap.
- ♥ Learn to play a musical instrument.
- ♥ Take a bath by candlelight. Scented candles make it extra-special!
- ♥ Listen to a new/different kind of music. For instance, if you like country-western, try opera. If you like classical, try jazz.
- ♥ Invite your friend for a walk.
- ♥ Buy yourself a pet to share life with.
- ♥ Visit a museum.
- ♥ Take a course in art appreciation or art history.
- ♥ Learn to use a computer or drive a car.
- ♥ Go to a planetarium.
- ♥ Go for a walk at night and see the stars.
- ♥ Spend a day at the beach. *(Try it sometime during the off-season.)*

- ♥ Take a hike or climb a mountain.
- ♥ Take a trip to a place you have always wanted to go.
- ♥ Invite a friend to a concert.
- ♥ Plant a flower or vegetable garden.
- ♥ Make a huge pot of soup and share it with someone elderly. (*I highly recommend this for people in mourning. There are many varied and easy soup recipes available in cookbooks. Soup is something that the elderly, the sick and people suffering grief can easily eat and digest. It is a healthy and a loving thing to do.*) ♥♥♥♥
- ♥ Do low-impact aerobics.
- ♥ Ride a bike or take a swim.
- ♥ Buy yourself a new cologne.
- ♥ Treat yourself to a facial—so relaxing.
- ♥ Go pick strawberries or apples or peaches at a farm.
- ♥ Try a new recipe.
- ♥ Try making strawberry jam or applesauce, or

canning peaches with all the extra produce picked at the farm.

- Bring a basket of berries to a friend.
- Learn about your town, city or state's history.
- Learn about your family's history; you might even become interested in genealogy.
- Read about the life of your favorite artist.
- Go to a ballet with a friend.
- Have a real tea—the way the British do—with a beautiful teapot, china cup and saucer, and maybe tea sandwiches.
- Use a pretty linen napkin with dinner.
- Make muffins and share with your neighbors.
- Write a letter or send a card to someone for no particular reason.
- Volunteer a few hours to your favorite charity, hospital, school, etc.
- Serve on the board of an organization that you admire.
- Try listening to a book on tape or CD.

- Go to a bookstore and find something wonderful.
- Try cappuccino at a coffeehouse and bring a book along to enjoy.
- Have a real picnic in your living room. Make all your favorite picnic foods, spread a cloth on the floor and go for it. (*This is lovely in front of a roaring fire in the middle of winter.*)
- Help weed a friend's garden.
- Try to do a crossword or a jigsaw puzzle. (*Beware, this can be frustrating, so pick an easy one.*)
- Go swing on a swing or play on a playground.
- Build a sandcastle or paint a picture.
- Get a museum coloring book and great colored markers or crayons. Pick a masterpiece and color it your way.
- Go to a ballgame and root, root, root for the home team.
- Brush your hair, fifty rhythmic strokes, and don't forget to include the back of your neck. (*Great for moving energies.*)

♥ Go on a garden tour.

♥ See an historic house; sometimes there may even be concerts.

♥ Sing in the shower.

♥ Pay a compliment to a stranger.

♥ Clean out a closet or junk drawer.

♥ Polish something. (*I like polishing silver and find it very relaxing and rewarding.*)

♥ Go to an outdoor café and people watch. Bring a sketch pad and doodle.

♥ Go to a card shop and read all the humorous cards. (Bet you'll smile!)

♥ Buy a bunch of picture postcards and send one a day to someone who needs cheering. (*This is especially nice for Alzheimer's patients because they can read the postcards many times. It's easy to write just a few lines a day, basically saying that you are thinking of them. I fill out all the addresses during TV commercial breaks and send them to people recuperating or in transitions. It is a very healing, loving thing to do.* **People love being bombarded with postcards.**) ♥♥♥♥♥♥♥♥

- ♥ Bring a jar of liquid bubbles to a children's park and blow bubbles galore. Be sure to bring extra wands to share.
- ♥ Do something you haven't done since childhood, like eat cotton candy, ride on a merry-go-round, build a large tower from wooden blocks.
- ♥ Take a course at your community college.
- ♥ Find out about Elder-hostel or Youth-hostel travel.
- ♥ Hold a hand.
- ♥ Hug someone.
- ♥ Thank someone for the nice things they have done.
- ♥ Go to a travel agency and pick up brochures about all the places you've dreamed about.
- ♥ Browse through a flea market or antiques shop.

- Write, or dictate, the story of your family.
- Write about your childhood.
- Send a bouquet of flowers to someone six months after the funeral. NOTE: *Do not send any flowers to a Jewish funeral or Jewish house in mourning. It is against the tradition. Send a fruit basket or kosher food platter instead.*
- Send a fruit basket to a house in mourning. (*I always include boxed juices, and I try to include something extra-special like pistachios or a can of fancy mixed nuts.*) NOTE: Fruit is acceptable to all religions with dietary laws.
- Plant a tree or have a tree planted in the memory of someone.
- Have a ritual meal by having each dish hold special meaning.
- Treat yourself to something.
- Read some fairy tales or folk tales from different countries.
- Give someone a small present.
- Return something you borrowed.
- Make yourself a cup of cocoa.

- ♥ Take a nap.
- ♥ Give yourself a compliment.
- ♥ Take a risk; have the courage to try something new!
- ♥ Read a poem aloud and enjoy the beauty of the words.
- ♥ Treat yourself to lunch out at your favorite restaurant.
- ♥ Visit your library.
- ♥ Forgive an old grievance; forget an old grudge.
- ♥ Give yourself a hug; you deserve it!
- ♥ List ten things you do well.
- ♥ Throw away something that you don't like.
- ♥ Laugh at yourself.

> *"If you can't laugh at yourself, you may be missing the joke of the century."*
> —DAME EDNA EVERAGE

- ♥ Enjoy silence—listen with your heart.
- ♥ Visit a shut-in; you'll both feel better.
- ♥ Try eating with chopsticks.

- Spend a day without TV.
- Learn a new craft: hook a rug, learn needlepoint, build a birdhouse.
- Organize some small corner of your life.
- Practice random acts of kindness.
- Go howl at the moon.

Remember: *"If you find a path with no obstacles, it probably doesn't lead anywhere."* —Unknown

I would like to leave you with these final thoughts:

Do all the good you can,

By all the means you can,

In all the ways you can,

In all the places you can,

At all the times you can,

To all the people you can,

As long as ever you can.

—JOHN WESLEY
Rules of Conduct